The Tatler

Voltaire

Translation by William F. Fleming

Contents

Dramatis Personæ

Euphemia.
Damis.
Hortensia.
Trasimon.
Clitander.
Nerine.
Pasquin.
Several Footmen belonging to Damis.

ACT I.

Euphemia, Damis.

Euphemia: Don't imagine, my dear, that, by what I'm going to say, I mean to exercise the authority of a mother, always ready as you know I am, to listen in my turn to your reasons when I think them good; my intention is not to lay my commands on you, but to give you my advice; it is my heart which speaks to you, and that experience I have had in the world makes me foresee evils which I would endeavor to prevent: you have been at court, I think, not above two months; believe me, 'tis a dangerous situation: the perfidious group of courtiers always look on a new-comer with an eye of malevolence, and soon find out all his imperfections: from the first moment, they condemn him, without pity or remorse; and, which is still worse, their judgment is irrevocable: be guarded against their malice: on the first step we take in life, the rest of it must in a great measure depend: if you once make yourself ridiculous, the world will think you always so: the impression will remain: it is in vain, as you advance in years, to change your conduct, and assume a more serious behavior: you will suffer a long time from old prejudices: even if we do grow better, we are still suspected; and I have often known men pay dearly in their old age for the errors of their youth: have a little regard therefore to the world, and remember you ought to live now more for that than for yourself.

Damis: Now I cannot conceive what all this long preamble tends to.

Euphemia: I see it appears to you both absurd and unnecessary: you despise those things which may be of the greatest consequence to you; one day or other perhaps you may believe me, when it will be too late: to be plain with you, you are indiscreet: my too long indulgence passed over this fault in your infancy, in your riper years I dread the effects of it: you are not without abilities, a good understanding, and a good heart; but, believe me, in a world so full of injustice, virtue will not make amends for vice; our faults are censured on every occasion, and perhaps the worst we can be guilty of is indiscretion: at court, my dear, the most necessary art is not to talk well, but to know how to hold one's tongue: this is not the place where society enjoys itself in the freedom of easy conversation; here they generally talk without saying anything, and the most tiresome babblers have the best success: I have been long acquainted with the court, and bad enough it is: but whilst we live there, we ought to conform to it. With regard to the women, you should be remarkably cautious; talk but seldom of them, and still less of yourself; pretend to be ignorant of all they do, and all they say; conceal your opinion, and disguise your sentiments; but, above all, be master of your secrets: he who tells those of another will always be esteemed a villain; and he who tells his own, be assured, will, here at least, be looked on as a fool. What have you to object to this?

Damis: Nothing: I am entirely of your opinion: I abominate the character of a tatler: that is not my foible, I assure you: so far from being guilty of the vice you seem to reproach me with, I now fairly confess to you, madam, that I have a long time concealed a thing from you which I ought to have told you of; but in life, you know, one must sometimes dissemble. I love, and am beloved, by a most charming widow, young, rich, and handsome, as prudent as she is amiable; in a word, it is Hortensia: judge, madam, yourself of my happiness; judge, if it were known, how miserable it would make all our courtiers, who are sighing for her: we have concealed our mutual passion from every one of them: this engagement has been made now for these two whole days past, and you knew nothing of it.

Euphemia: But I have been at Paris all that time.

Damis: O madam, never was man so happy in his choice: the more you approve of it, the more satisfaction shall I feel, and the more pleasure in my pursuit of her.

Euphemia: I am sure, Damis, the confidence you repose in me, is a mark of your friendship, and not of your imprudence.

Damis: I hope you never doubted that.

Euphemia: But seriously, Damis, you should reflect on the prospect of happiness before you: Hortensia, I know, has charms, but, besides that, she is the best match that could have offered itself in all France.

Damis: I know she is.

Euphemia: She is entirely her own mistress, and can choose for herself.

Damis: So much the better.

Euphemia: You must take care how you manage her, mark her inclinations, and flatter them.

Damis: O I can do better: I know how to please her.

Euphemia: Well said, Damis: but remember, she's not fond of noise and bustle; no blustering or flashy airs will be agreeable to her: she may, like other women, have her foibles, but even in love matters she'll always act with discretion: above all, let me advise you not to show off in public with her, nor appear at court together, as if on purpose to be stared at, and become the topic of the day: secret and mystery are all her taste.

Damis: And yet the affair must be known at last.

Euphemia: But, pray, what lucky accident introduced you to her? she never admits young men to her toilette; but, like a prudent woman, carefully avoids the crowd of wild sparks that are perpetually after her.

Damis: To tell you the truth, I have never been at her house yet: but I have ogled her a long time, and, thank heaven, with success: at first she sent back my letters unopened, but soon after read them, and now writes to me again: for near two days past I have had strong hopes, and, in a word, intend this very night to have a tête-à-tête with her.

Euphemia: Well: I think I'll go and see her, too: the mother of a lover who is well received, cannot, I imagine, but be agreeable to her. I may contrive to speak of you, and prevail on her to hasten the match, on which I shall tell her your happiness depends: get her consent, and make her yours as soon as you can; I'll do my best to assist you: but speak of it to nobody else, I charge you.

Damis: No, madam: never was mother more tender and affectionate, or friendship more sincere; and to please her shall, for the future, be my first ambition.

Euphemia: All that I desire of you is, to be happy.

SCENE II.

Damis: [Alone.] My mother is right: address and cunning are absolutely necessary in this world; there is no succeeding without them. I am resolved to dissemble with the whole court, except ten or a dozen friends, whom I may talk freely with: but first, by way of trial of my prudence, let me tell my secrets to myself a little, and consider, now nobody's by, what fortune has bestowed on me. I hate vanity, but there's no harm in knowing one's self, and doing ourselves justice: I have some wit, am agreeable, well received at court, and thought, I believe, by some, to be admitted to the king's private hours: then, I am certainly very handsome, can dance, sing, drink, and dissemble with the best of them: made a colonel at thirteen, I have reason to hope for a staff at thirty; happy in what I have, and with a good prospect before me; I'll keep Julia, and marry Hortensia; when I have possessed her charms, I'll be guilty every day of a thousand infidelities, but all with prudence and economy, and without ever being suspected as a rambler: in six months' time I shall make away with half her fortune, and enjoy all the court by turns, without her knowing anything of the matter.

SCENE III.

Damis, Trasimon.

Damis: Good morrow, governor.

Trasimon: [Aside.] Hang him for coming across me.

Damis: My dear governor, let me embrace thee.

Trasimon: Excuse me, sir, but I really—

Damis: Positively I will: come, come—

Trasimon: Well, what, what do you want?

Damis: Nay, don't frown so, man, pray thee unbend a little: I am the happiest of mortals.

Trasimon: I came to tell you, sir—

Damis: O by heavens, you kill me with that hard frozen face of yours!

Trasimon: I can't help it, sir, nor can I smile at present, for, let me tell you, you have got a bad affair upon your hands.

Damis: Not so very bad, surely.

Trasimon: Erminia and Valere exclaim violently against you: you have spoke of them, it seems, too lightly, and old Lord Horace too desired me to tell you—

Damis: O a mighty matter indeed to be uneasy about! Horace, an old lord! an old fool, a proud coxcomb, puffed up with notions of false honor, low enough at court, he puts on an air of importance in the city, and is as ignorant as he would fain seem knowing: as for Madam Erminia, it's pretty well known I had her, and left her abruptly, an ill-natured busybody; I believe you know a little of her lover, my friend, Valere; did you ever remember such a starched, affected, strained, left-handed understanding? O by the by, I was told yesterday in confidence, that his huge elder brother, that important creature, is well received by Clarice, and the fat countess is bursting with spleen and disappointment. Well but, my old commandant, how go your love-affairs?

Trasimon: You know I don't trouble myself much about the sex.

Damis: That's not my case; for I do, and in faith, both in court and city, they keep me pretty well employed: but listen, while I intrust you with a secret, on which the happiness of my life depends.

Trasimon: Can I serve you in it?

Damis: No: not in the least.

Trasimon: Then pray tell me nothing about it.

Damis: O but the rights of friendship—

Trasimon: 'Tis that very friendship which makes me shrink from the weight of a secret which is intrusted to me, not out of real regard, but from mere folly and weakness, which anybody else might keep as well as myself; which is generally attended with a thousand suspicions, and may chance to give us both a great deal of uneasiness, me for knowing, and you for saying more than you ought.

Damis: Say what you will about it, captain, I must let you have the pleasure of reading this billet-doux, which this very day—

Trasimon: What a strange humor—

Damis: You'll say it's written with a great deal of tenderness.

Trasimon: Well, if you insist upon it—

Damis: 'Tis dictated by love itself: you'll see how fond she is of me: 'tis the hand that wrote it which makes it so valuable: but you shall see it: zounds, I've lost it; positively I can't find it—hullo, la Fleur, la Brie.

SCENE IV.

Damis, Trasimon, Several Footmen.

Footman: Did you call, sir?

Damis: Step immediately into the gallery, and bring me all the letters I received this morning: go to the old duke, and—O here it is, the blundering rascals had put it there by mistake. [To the footman] you may go. Now, you shall see it; mind now, I beg you'll attend.

SCENE V.

Damis, Trasimon, Clitander, Pasquin.

Clitander: [With a letter in his hand, speaking to Pasquin.]

Stay you, Pasquin, in this garden all day; be sure you mark everything that passes; observe Hortensia well; and bring me an account of every step she takes: I shall know then—

SCENE VI.

Damis, Trasimon, Clitander.

Damis: O here comes the marquis: good morrow, marquis.

Clitander: [A letter in his hand.] Morrow to you.

Damis: Why, what's the matter with you to-day, with that long melancholy face? what the deuce ails you all? every creature I see looks gloomy and dismal to-day, I think; but I suppose—

Clitander: [Aside.] I have but too much reason.

Damis: What are you muttering about?

Clitander: [In a low voice.] What a poor unhappy creature I am!

Damis: Come, to give you both a little spirit, suppose I read you this little billet of mine, ha, marquis?

Clitander: [Aside, looking at the letter.] What letter? can it be? surely 'tis from Hortensia: cruel creature!

Damis: [To Clitander.] 'Tis a letter would make a rival hang himself.

Clitander: You are indeed a happy man, if you are beloved.

Damis: That I most assuredly am; but you shall hear; your city ladies don't write in this style: observe her. [He reads] "At length I yield to the passion which has taken possession of my heart; I would have concealed it, but 'tis impossible: why should I not write what my eyes, no doubt, have a thousand times informed you of? yes, my dearest Damis, I own I love you; the more perhaps because my heart, fearful of your youth, and fearful of itself, for a long time resisted my inclination, and told me I ought not to love you. After the confession of such a weakness, ought I not forever to reproach myself for it? but the more frankly I avow my tenderness for you, with the more care you ought to conceal it."

Trasimon: You take care, I see, to obey the lady's commands most punctually: a mighty discreet lover, to be sure!

Clitander: Happy is that man who receives such letters, and never shows them.

Damis: Well, what do you think of it? is it not—

Trasimon: Very strong indeed.

Clitander: Charming.

Damis: And the writer a thousand times more so. O if you did but know her name! but in this wicked world we must have a little discretion.

Trasimon: Well, we don't desire you to tell us.

Clitander: You and I, Damis, love one another very well, but prudence—

Trasimon: So far from desiring you to acquaint us with particulars, that—

Damis: Come, come, I love you both, too well to dissemble with you: I know, you think, and the whole court has proclaimed it, that I have no affair here with anybody but Julia.

Clitander: Nay, they have it from yourself; but as to us, we do not believe a word of it.

Damis: To be sure, there was something between us, and the affair went on tolerably well till now: we loved one another, and then we parted, and then we met again; all the world knows that.

Clitander: The world, I assure you, knows nothing at all about it.

Damis: You think I'm very fond of her still, but you're mistaken; upon honor I am not.

Trasimon: 'Tis nothing to me, whether you are or are not.

Damis: Julia is handsome, that she is; but then she's fickle: the other—O the other is the very thing!

Clitander: Well, and this charming woman—

Damis: Come, I see you will know, and I must tell you: my dear friend, look at this picture, only look at it: did you ever see two such eyes? the most charming, most adorable creature; painted by Mace; that you know is saying everything; you know the features, don't you?

Clitander: O heaven! 'tis Hortensia.

Damis: You seem surprised.

Trasimon: You forget, sir, that Hortensia is my cousin, that she is tender of her honor, and a declaration of this kind—

Damis: O give her up, give her up, man; why, I have six cousins; you shall have them all: make up to them, ogle them, deceive them, desert them, print their love-letters, with all my heart, it will give me no uneasiness: we should have enough to do indeed to be out of humor with one another, to vindicate the honor of our cousins: it's very well here, if every one can answer for themselves.

Trasimon: But Hortensia, sir—

Damis: Is the woman I adore; and I tell you again, sir, she loves me, and me only; and to make you more angry, I intend to marry her.

Clitander: [Aside.] Could I have been more cruelly injured?

Damis: Our wedding will be no secret, but you shan't be there—cousin.

Trasimon: A cousin, sir may have some power over her, and that you shall know soon. Your servant, sir.

SCENE VII.

Damis, Clitander.

Damis: How I detest that fellow! the ridiculous pedant, with his affected airs of romantic virtue; a tedious, heavy, tiresome brute! you seem to be mighty curious about that picture, and examine it closely.

Clitander: [Aside.] I must be master of myself, and dissemble.

Damis: You may observe perhaps, one of the brilliants is missing at the corner there. It was a long chase yesterday, and there was such jostling and pushing one another; you must know I had four pictures loose in my pocket, and this unfortunately met with a mischance; the case broke, and a brilliant dropped out: as you go to town to-morrow, you may call at Frénaye's, he's dear, but clever in his way: I wish you'd choose a diamond at his shop, as if it was for yourself; for, between you and me, I owe him a few pounds: here, take the picture, but don't show it to anybody. Your servant.

Clitander: [Aside.] Where am I?

Damis: Well, God be with you, marquis, I shall depend on you. Take care, be discreet now.

Clitander: [Aside.] Can he possibly do it?

Damis: [Returning.] I love a discreet friend: you shall be my confidant: I'll tell you all my secrets. Is it possible for a man to be happy, to possess everything his heart can wish for, and not tell it to another? where's the joy of keeping our insipid pleasures to ourselves? one may as well have no friends as not trust them, and happiness uncommunicated is no happiness at all: I have shown you a letter, and a picture, but that's not all.

Clitander: Why, what else have you?

Damis: Do you know that this very night I am to meet her?

Clitander: [Aside.] O dreadful! horrible!

Damis: To-night, Clitander, before the ball is over, alone and unsuspected, I am to meet her by appointment in this garden.

Clitander: [Aside.] O I am lost, undone: this last cruel stroke—

Damis: Is not that charming, my friend? dost not rejoice with me, boy?

Clitander: And will Hortensia meet you?

Damis: Most certainly; just at dusk I expect her; but the declining sun already gives me notice of my approaching happiness: I must be gone. I'll go to your lodgings, I think, and dress: let me see, I must have two pounds of powder for my hair, and some of the most exquisite perfume; then will I return in triumph, and finish the affair immediately. Do you, in the meantime, prowl about here, that you may have some share in the happiness of your friend; I shall leave you here as my deputy, to keep off impertinent rivals.

SCENE VIII.

Clitander: [Alone.] How hard a task it was to conceal my grief and my resentment! after a whole year of sincerest passion, when Hortensia's heart, wearied of resistance, began at length to soften and relent, for Damis thus to come and change her in an instant! one fortunate moment has done what my long and faithful services in vain solicited: nay, she even anticipated his wishes, gave this young coxcomb that picture which I had so much better deserved: she writes to him, too! O that letter would have killed me with ecstasy: and then, to make my misery complete, she has written to me this morning, never to see her more: this hair-brained fellow has got hold of her heart, and will carry her off in triumph: O Hortensia, how cruelly hast thou deceived me!

SCENE IX.

Clitander, Pasquin.

Clitander: So, Pasquin, I have found out my rival.

Pasquin: Indeed, sir? so much the worse.

Clitander: Yes: she's in love with that blockhead, Damis.

Pasquin: Who told you so?

Clitander: Himself: the proud coxcomb boasted to me of the treasure he had stolen from me. Here, Pasquin, look at this picture; out of mere vanity he has left it in my hands, only that he may triumph the more. O Hortensia, who could ever have believed that Damis would supplant Clitander!

Pasquin: Damis is a good and pretty fellow.

Clitander: [Collaring him.] Ha! rascal, an impertinent young fool, that—

Pasquin: Very true, sir, and perhaps—but, for heaven's sake, don't strangle me, sir: between you and me, sir, he's nothing but a babbler, a prig—

Clitander: Be he what he will, she prefers him to me, Pasquin; therefore now is the time to exert thy usual skill, and serve me. Hortensia and my rival are to meet this night in the garden, by appointment; find out some method, if possible, to prevent it.

Pasquin: But, sir—

Clitander: Thy brain, I know, is fertile; take money, as much as thou wilt: for heaven's sake, disappoint my rival: while he is tricking out his insignificant person, we may rob him of the happy moment: since he is a fool, let us take the advantage of his folly, and by some means or other keep him away from this place.

Pasquin: And this you think mighty easy to be done: why, sir, I would sooner engage to stop the course of a river, a stag on a heath, or a bird in the air, a mad poet repeating his own verses, a litigious woman that has a suit in chancery, a parson hunting after a benefice, a high-wind, a tempest, or thunder and lightning, than a young coxcomb going to a rendezvous with his mistress.

Clitander: And will you then abandon me to despair?

Pasquin: Stay: a thought is just come into my head: let me see, Hortensia and Damis have never seen me?

Clitander: Never.

Pasquin: You have got her picture?

Clitander: I have.

Pasquin: Good: and you have got a letter that she wrote you.

Clitander: Ay, and a cruel one it is.

Pasquin: Her ladyship's orders, I think, to you, never to visit her again.

Clitander: It is so.

Pasquin: The letter is without a direction I think?

Clitander: It is, rascal, and what of that?

Pasquin: Give me the picture and the letter immediately; give them me, I say.

Clitander: Shall I give a picture into other hands that was intrusted to my care?

Pasquin: Come, come, no ceremony: a pretty scruple indeed! give them me.

Clitander: Well, but Pasquin—

Pasquin: Leave everything to me, and rely on my discretion.

Clitander: You want to—

Pasquin: Away, away: here comes Hortensia.

SCENE X.

Hortensia, Nerine.

Hortensia: What you say, Nerine, is very true; Clitander is a worthy man; I know the warmth of his passion for me, and the sincerity of it: he is sober, sensible, constant, and discreet: I ought to esteem him, and so I do; but Damis is my taste: I find, by the struggles of my own heart, that love is not always the reward of virtue; we are always won by an agreeable outside; and for one who is captivated by the perfections of the soul, a thousand are caught by the eye; I blush at my own inconstancy: but Damis comes no more here, I assure you.

Nerine: What a strange humor this is! how resolute you are!

Hortensia: No: I ought not to be there first, and positively I will not.

Nerine: Are you afraid of the first meeting?

Hortensia: To tell you the truth, Damis takes up all my thoughts: this very day I have had a visit from his mother, who has greatly increased my prejudices in favor of her son: I see she is extremely eager for the match, and presses it in the warmest manner: but I want to see the man himself in private, and sound his real sentiments.

Nerine: You have no doubt of his regard for you?

Hortensia: None: I believe, nay, I know he loves me; but I want to hear him tell me so a thousand and a thousand times over: I want to see if he deserves my love, to know his temper, his character, and his heart: I would not yield blindly to inclination, but judge of him, if I could, without passion or prejudice.

SCENE XI.

Hortensia, Nerine, Pasquin.

Pasquin: Madam, my master Damis has sent me here to acquaint you privately—

Hortensia: Is he not coming himself?

Pasquin: No, madam.

Nerine: The little villain!

Hortensia: Not come to me?

Pasquin: No, madam: but, as in point of honor he thinks himself obliged, he has sent you back this portrait.

Hortensia: My picture!

Pasquin: Please to take it, madam.

Hortensia: Am I awake?

Pasquin: Pray, ma'am, make haste, for I am really in a hurry: I have two more pictures to carry back for my master, and two to receive: and so, madam, till we meet again, I am your most obsequious—

Hortensia: Perfidious wretch! I shall die with grief.

Pasquin: He desired me, moreover, madam, to inform you, that you need not ogle him any more, and that for the future he should be glad if you would find out some other dupe to laugh at besides himself.

S
CENE XII.

Hortensia, Nerine, Damis, Pasquin.

Damis: [At the farther end of the stage.] Here I am to meet the dear object of my wishes.

Pasquin: Ha! Damis! then I am caught; but I'll take courage, however, and proceed. [He runs up to Damis and takes him aside.] I belong, sir, to Lady Hortensia, and have the honor to be employed on her little affairs; I have, sir, here a billet-doux for you.

Hortensia: What a change is here! what a reward for my tender passion!

Damis: [Reads.] Let me see, ha! how's this? "You deserve my regard, I know the esteem that is due to your virtues, but I cannot love you." Was ever such abominable perfidy? this is what I little expected indeed; but it shall be known; the public shall be acquainted with it: it shall be no secret at court, I can assure her.

Hortensia: [At the other part of the stage.] Could he carry his infamous perfidy so far as this?

Damis: There, madam, you see what value I set on your correspondence. [He tears the letter.]

Pasquin: [Running up to Hortensia.] O madam, I blush for his behavior: you saw him tear the letter, which you condescended to write to the ungrateful man.

Hortensia: He has sent back my picture: perish, thou wretched image of my ineffectual charms! [She throws down the picture.]

Pasquin: [Coming back to Damis.] There, sir, you see how she treats you; she has thrown away your picture, and broken it in pieces.

Damis: There are some ladies in the world who receive the original in a very different manner, I can assure her.

Hortensia: O Nerine, what a regard I had for this ungrateful man! Tell me, fellow, [Speaking to Pasquin, andgiving him money] for whose sake is it I am thus deserted? to what happy object am I sacrificed?

Pasquin: O madam, to five or six beauties, with whom he pretends to be in love, though he cares as little for them as for yourself; but your most dangerous rival is the fair Julia.

Damis: [Coming up to Pasquin.] Here, take this ring, and now tell me honestly, on what impertinent court fool your sweet mistress has fixed her affections.

Pasquin: No one, sir, deserves her so well as yourself; but, to tell you the truth, there is a certain young abbé who ogles her perpetually; not to mention that I frequently help her cousin Trasimon over the garden-wall of an evening.

Damis: I'm glad of it: this is excellent news; I'll put it into a ballad.

Hortensia: The worst of it is, Nerine, that to make me still more unhappy, this affair will make a noise in the world, and I shall be horribly exposed: come, let us be gone, I will retire, and hide my tears.

Pasquin: [To Hortensia.] You have no more commands for me, madam? [To Damis] Can I be of any further service to you, sir? Heaven preserve you both!

SCENE XIII.

Hortensia, Damis, Nerine.

Hortensia: [Returning.] Why do I stay in this place?

Damis: I ought to be dancing at the ball now.

Hortensia: He seems thoughtful, but 'tis not on my account.

Damis: I am mistaken, or she looks this way; I'll even make up to her.

Hortensia: I'll avoid him.

Damis: O stay, Hortensia, can you fly me, can you avoid me? cruel, perfidious woman!

Hortensia: Ungrateful man, leave me to myself, and let me try to hate you.

Damis: That, madam, will be an easy task, thanks to your infidelity.

Hortensia: 'Tis what I ought to do: 'tis but my duty now, thanks to your injustice.

Damis: And are we met at last, Hortensia, but to quarrel?

Hortensia: How can Damis talk thus, and at the same time affront me, and love another! O Julia, Julia!

Damis: After your writing me such a letter, madam—

Hortensia: After your sending back my picture, sir—

Damis: Could I send back your picture? cruel woman!

Hortensia: Could I ever write a line to you that was not full of love and tenderness? perfidious man!

Damis: Madam, I will consent to leave the court, to give up the posts I enjoy, and all my hopes of future preferment, to be despised and condemned by the whole world, if ever I sent you back the picture, the precious treasure which love intrusted to my care.

Hortensia: And may I never be loved by the dear charmer of my soul, if I ever sent you that letter! but here, here, ungrateful man, is the picture your insolence returned me, the reward of tender friendship, which you despised; 'tis here, and can you—

Damis: Ha! here comes Clitander.

SCENE XIV.

Hortensia, Damis, Clitander, Nerine, Pasquin.

Damis: My dear marquis, come here; where are you going? He, madam, will unravel all.

Hortensia: Clitander? why, what does he know of the matter?

Damis: Don't be alarmed, madam, he is my friend, to whom I have opened my whole heart: he is my confidant, let him be yours too: you must, indeed you must.

Hortensia: Let us be gone this moment, Nerine: O heaven! what a ridiculous creature!

SCENE XV.

Damis, Clitander, Pasquin.

Damis: O marquis, I am the most unhappy of men; let me speak to you; I must follow her: observe me. [To Hortensia] Stay, Hortensia; nay, then I must after her.

Scene Xvi.

Clitander, Pasquin.

Clitander: I don't know what to think of it, Pasquin; I understood, by what you told me, that they had quarrelled.

Pasquin: I thought so, too: I'm sure I played my part: most certainly they have cause to hate one another; but, for aught I know, a minute's time may reconcile them again.

Clitander: Let us observe which way they turn.

Pasquin: Hortensia seems as if she was going to her own house.

Clitander: Damis follows her close: by his being behind, however, it looks as if she shunned him.

Pasquin: She flies but slowly, and the lover pursues.

Clitander: She turns her head back, and Damis talks to her, but to no purpose.

Pasquin: I fancy not, but Damis stops her often.

Clitander: He kneels to her, but she treats him with contempt.

Pasquin: O but observe, now she looks tenderly on him: if so, you're undone.

Clitander: She is gone into her own house, and has dismissed him: joy and fear, hope and despair, at once surround me; I can't imagine how it will end.

SCENE XVII.

clitander, damis, pasquin.

Damis: O my dear marquis, I'm glad you're here; for heaven's sake, inform me, what can be the meaning that Hortensia forbids my coming nigh her? how happens it that the picture, which I trusted to you, is now in her hands? answer me.

Clitander: You amaze and confound me.

Damis: [To Pasquin.] As for you, sir rascal there, the servant of Hortensia, at least the pretended, one, I'll make an end of you this moment.

Pasquin: [To Clitander.] Protect me, sir.

Clitander: [To Damis.] Well, sir—

Damis: 'Tis in vain—

Clitander: Spare this poor fellow, let me entreat you, do.

Damis: What interest have you in him?

Clitander: I beg of you, and seriously.

Damis: Out of regard to you, I will withhold my resentment; but tell me, scoundrel, the whole black contrivance.

Pasquin: O sir, 'tis a most mysterious affair; but I'll let you into some surprising secrets, if you'll promise not to reveal them.

Damis: I'll promise nothing, and insist on knowing all.

Pasquin: You shall, sir, but Hortensia is coming this way, and will overhear us. [To Clitander] Come, sir, let us to the masquerade, and there I'll tell you everything.

SCENE XVIII.

Trasimon, Nerine, Hortensiain a Domino, with a Masque in Her Hand.

Trasimon: Take my word for it, Hortensia, this young coxcomb will cover us with shame and ignominy, to show your letters and your picture about in this public manner: 'tis intolerable: I saw them myself; but I'll punish the scoundrel as he deserves.

Hortensia: [To Nerine.] Is Julia then so beautiful in his eyes? do you think he's really in love with her?

Trasimon: No matter whether he is or no: but, if he dishonors you, it concerns me nearly; I know a relative's duty, and will perform it.

Hortensia: [To Nerine.] Do you imagine he is engaged to Julia? give me your opinion.

Nerine: One may know that easily enough from himself.

Hortensia: O Nerine, he was excessively indiscreet; I ought to hate, yet perhaps still love him. O how he wept, and swore he loved, that he adored me, and that he would conceal our mutual passion!

Trasimon: There, I'm sure, he promised more than he will perform.

Hortensia: For the last time, however, I mean to try him: he's gone to the masquerade, there I shall be sure to find him: you must dissemble, Nerine: go and tell him that Julia expects him here with impatience: this masque at least will hide my blushes: the faithless man will take me for Julia: I shall know what he thinks of her, and of myself: on this meeting will depend my choice or my contempt of him. [To Trasimon.] You must not be far off: endeavor if you can, to keep Clitander near you: wait for me here, or hereabouts, and I will call you when there is occasion.

SCENE XIX.

Hortensia: [Alone, in a domino, with a masque in her hand.] At length it is time to fix my wavering affections; under the cover of this masque, and the name of Julia, I shall know whether his indiscretion was owing to excess of love, or vanity; whether I ought to pardon, or to detest him: but here he comes.

SCENE XX.

Hortensia Masqued, Damis.

Damis: [Not seeing Hortensia.] This seems to be the favorite spot for ladies to make their assignations in: well, I'll follow the fashion: fashion, in France, determines everything, regulates precedency, honor, good-breeding, merit, wit, and pleasure.

Hortensia: [Aside.] The coxcomb!

Damis: If this affair of mine could but be known, in two years' time the whole court would run mad for love of me: a good setting out here is everything: then Ægle, and Doris, and—O there's no counting them, such a group, such a sweet prospect! O the pretty creatures—

Hortensia: [Aside.] Light, vain man!

Damis: O Julia, is it you? I know you in spite of that envious masque: my heart cannot be mistaken; come, come, my dear Julia, take off that cruel veil that hides thy beauties from me; do not, in pity do not, conceal those sweet looks, those tender smiles, that were meant to reward that love which they inspired; thou art the only woman on earth whom I adore.

Hortensia: Let me tell you, Damis, you are a stranger to my humor and disposition; I should despise a heart that never felt for any woman but myself; I like my lovers should be more fashionable; that twenty young flirts should be hunting after him; that his passion for me should draw him away from a hundred contending beauties; I must have some noble sacrifice offered up to me, or I'll never accept of his services: a lover less esteemed would be of no value, I should despise him.

Damis: I can make you easy on that head, my dear; I have made some pretty good conquests, and perhaps as expeditiously as most men: I believe I can boast of tolerable success that way: many a fine woman has run after me; another man would be vain of it: I could reckon up a few of your nice ladies who are not over-coy with me.

Hortensia: Well, but who, who are they?

Damis: Only give the word, my Julia, and I begin the sacrifice: there is, first, the little Isabel; secondly, the lively, smart Erminia; then there's Clarice, Ægle, Doris—

Hortensia: Poor, pitiful offerings! I could have a hundred such every day: these will never do: they are loved, and turned off again twenty times in a week: let me have some respectable names, women of character, such as I may triumph over without a blush: if you could reckon among your captives, one, who, before she saw the incomparable Damis, was invulnerable, one who in all actions paid the strictest regard to decency and decorum, some modest, prudent fair, who never felt a weakness but for you, that would be the woman.

Damis: [Sitting down by her.] Now then, observe me: I have a mistress who exactly resembles in every feature the picture you have drawn: but you would not have me be so indiscreet as to—

Hortensia: Not for the world.

Damis: If I were imprudent enough to tell her name, I should call her—Hortensia. Why are you startled at it? I think not of her while my Julia's here: she is neither young nor handsome when you are by: besides, there is a certain young abbé who is very familiar with her; and, between you and me, her cousin Trasimon is too apt to come to her in an evening over the garden-wall.

Hortensia: [Aside.] To join calumny thus to his infidelity, execrable villain! but I must dissemble: pray, Damis, on what footing are you with Hortensia? does she love you?

Damis: O to distraction, that's the truth of it.

Hortensia: [Aside.] Impudence and falsehood to the highest degree!

Damis: 'Tis even so, I assure you, I would not tell you a lie for the world.

Hortensia: [Aside.] The villain!

Damis: But what signifies thinking about her? we did not meet here to talk of Hortensia: come, let us rather—

Hortensia: I can never believe Hortensia would ever have given herself up so totally to you.

Damis: I tell you, I have it under her own hand.

Hortensia: I don't believe a word of it.

Damis: 'Tis insulting me to doubt it.

Hortensia: Let me see it then.

Damis: You injure me, madam: there, read, perhaps you know her hand. [Gives her the letter.]

Hortensia: [Unmasking.] I do, villain, and know your treachery: at length I have in some measure atoned for my folly, and have luckily recovered both the picture and the letter, which I had ventured to trust in such unworthy hands: 'tis done: now Trasimon and Clitander, appear.

SCENE XXI.

Hortensia, Damis, Trasimon, Clitander.

Hortensia: [To Clitander.] If I have not yet offended you beyond a possibility of pardon; if you can still love Hortensia, my hand, my fortune, and my life are yours.

Clitander: O Hortensia, behold at your feet a despairing lover, who receives your kind offer with joy and transport.

Trasimon: [To Damis.] Did I not tell you, sir, I should bring her to a right way of thinking? this marriage, sir, is my making: now, Damis, fare you well, and henceforth, learn to dissemble better or never attempt it more.

Damis: Just heaven! for the future how shall I venture to speak at all?

End.

www.ingramcontent.com/pod-product-compliance
Lightning Source LLC
Chambersburg PA
CBHW021123020426

42331CB00004B/610